Successful Selling

Successful Selling

Christine Harvey

BARRON'S

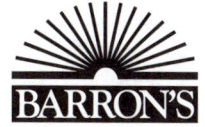

First U.S. edition © copyright 1999 by
Barron's Educational Series, Inc.

Previously published in 1998 in Great Britain by
Hodder and Stoughton Educational, copyright © 1992,
1998 Christine Harvey

All rights reserved.

No part of this book may be reproduced in any form, by
photostat, microfilm, xerography, or any other means, or
incorporated into any information retrieval system, electronic
or mechanical, without the written permission of the
copyright owner.

All inquiries should be addressed to:
Barron's Educational Series, Inc.
250 Wireless Boulevard
Hauppauge, New York 11788
http://www.barronseduc.com

Library of Congress Catalog Card Number 98-45321

International Standard Book No. 0-7641-1055-1

Library of Congress Cataloging-in-Publication Data
Harvey, Christine.
 [Successful selling in a week]
 Successful selling / Successful selling in a week
   p. cm. — (A business success guide)
 Includes index.
 ISBN 0-7641-1055-1
 1. Selling. I. Title. II. Series
 HF5438.25.H385 1999
 658.85—dc21   98-45321
                                                     CIP

PRINTED IN HONG KONG
9 8 7 6 5 4 3 2 1

Contents

Introduction v

Chapter 1
Plan Your Success 1

Chapter 2
Gaining Product and Service Expertise 11

Chapter 3
Discover the Buying Motives 21

Chapter 4
Overcome Objections 33

Chapter 5
Presentations and Closings 45

Chapter 6
Action-Provoking Systems 57

Chapter 7
Self-Motivation and Support Systems 69

Chapter 8
Summarizing Successful Selling 81

Index 85

Introduction

◆

Selling as an occupation is something that leaves most people terror-stricken. Yet selling is such an integral part of running any business that good salespeople are in great demand.

Successful selling is *not* a "fly-by-the-seat-of-the-pants" process. It is, in fact, a structured set of systems that all professional high achievers learn.

Each chapter of this book looks at one of the seven steps to successful selling:

- ◆ Plan your success
- ◆ Product and service knowledge
- ◆ Discover the buying motives
- ◆ Overcome objections and use them to your advantage
- ◆ Presentations and closings
- ◆ Action-provoking systems
- ◆ Self-motivation and support systems

Successful selling brings with it high success, career progression, self-satisfaction, and personal growth.

Chapter 1

Plan Your Success

Let's look at the elements of preparation required for a successful approach to selling:

- Set overall goal
- Break the goal into daily work segments
- Carry out these daily segments
- Gain prospective customers
- Spend time on critical activities
- Create self-management system charts
- Organize work systems

SET OVERALL GOAL

Start at the top of the list and set your goals. What do you want to achieve? Calculate it in some specific terms. Will it be a monetary figure, a percentage or multiple of a target set by your company, a possession to be acquired, or even a promotion?

Now think about how to convert that goal to the actual number of sales you need in order to achieve your target. Now the next step is critical and this is the step most unsuccessful salespeople avoid. Divide your total sales into weekly and daily sales and then calculate the work necessary to achieve that.

◆ Plan Your Success

CALCULATE WORKLOAD

- ◆ How many sales do I want? _____
- ◆ How many prospects will I need to see in order to make one sale? _____
- ◆ How many prospects do I need in order to reach my total sales target? _____
- ◆ How many activities do I need to do to generate one prospect?
  — Telephone calls _____
  — Direct mail letters _____
  — Exhibitions or seminars _____
  — Advertisements _____
  — Cold calling _____
  — Other _____
- ◆ What daily activity schedule and results do I have to maintain in order to achieve my goal? (Include visits, telephone calls, and all of the above.)

  _____
  _____
  _____
  _____
  _____
  _____

SELF-DECEPTION

Bob Broadley, one of the world's top insurance salespeople, says that the single biggest failure salespeople make is *self-deception*. He said he wasn't "born with success." He had to study the most successful salespeople he could find.

His advice? "Don't fool yourself into thinking you're selling when you're not in front of the right number of people every day. Working eight hours per day is not the point. It's what you do in those eight hours that counts."

If you're not in front of enough prospects, you won't sell enough to make your target. And how do you get in front of enough prospects? By making enough appointments. It's that straightforward. "Yet many people fool themselves by thinking they are selling when in fact they are doing busy work," says Bob.

Remember, the difference between success and failure often is neglecting to break down the overall target into daily targets and tasks.

Let's look at advice from people who succeed year after year. How do they put this principle into practice?

♦ Plan Your Success

One salesman with a worldwide reputation for success is Ove Sjögren from Electrolux in Sweden. He has calculated his yearly target and broken it down into a daily figure. He knows exactly how many sales he must make per day. He knows how many prospects he must see each day.

He stresses that staying at the top is easy if you know how much you must do every day and you do it.

NOT ME!

"Oh, daily targets don't relate to me," many people argue. That's the biggest misconception I hear from seminar delegates. They really believe they can't break *their* activity into daily targets.

This is the first mental change you must make if you are to succeed in selling. Sales come about from methodically carrying out the right practices, day in and day out.

Whether you sell large systems to governments that require three years to close, or retail products to customers that take three minutes to close, you still have to calculate *which* daily component parts will lead you to success. Even if you only want three customers per year, you'll have to negotiate with six, nine, or twelve prospects constantly. You need to know *how many* and keep this running *constantly*.

CREATE DAILY SEGMENTS

Why do we put so much stress on daily sales targets and daily activity targets? It's because we've seen so many failures by talented, hard-working, well-meaning people who deserved to succeed. No one ever sat them down and said, "Look, success comes by doing the right number of activities day in and day out."

MAKE REMINDERS

You are reading this book in order to succeed. You want to use a strategic approach. You want to avoid the pitfalls of others. Therefore, take today to plan your targets. Plan your systems for reaching your targets. Draw up wall charts, pocket memos—anything and everything you need to remind yourself that hard work alone will not bring you success. It's a matter of scheduling and seeing the right number of people today as well as carrying out specific activities that will allow you to see the right number of people tomorrow.

CALCULATE

What is the right number? If you need one sale per day and you have to see three prospects in order to convert one to a sale, then you need three sales visits per day. That's if you can do one-call closings; in other words, you only need to see each prospect once. But what if you need to see each prospect twice on average and you need to make one sale per day? How many sales visits will you need to do every day? Six.

1 sale × 3 prospects × 2 visits = 6 visits per day

You'll need time for making appointments, and following up on promises you make during the appointments. Therefore, the need for planning your targets and breaking them into daily workloads is essential.

IS "YOUR BEST" A MEASURE?

What if you didn't do the calculation? What if you just worked as hard as you could? What do you think the result would be?

Perhaps this example will help. On one of my speaking engagements in Singapore, a journalist approached me and asked, "Why do you so often stress the importance of daily targets? Isn't it enough for people to just do their best?"

"Look at it this way," I suggested. "What if you were training to be an Olympic champion runner? Would you go out every day and practice running any distance at any speed, just doing your best? Or would you know exactly how far you had to run and at what speed you had to run in order to meet your defined goal?"

"Oh yes, I see," she responded. It seemed to click for her. It's painful for people to work hard and do their best, to have high expectations and then be let down. However, with daily targets set, you are able to work with focus and purpose. You won't fail by thinking sales will come to you magically, suddenly or later.

PITFALLS FOR BUSINESS OWNERS TOO

New business owners have exactly the same problem, and you can learn from them. Here's an example. Two very talented young dress designers with their own shop asked advice for succeeding in their business. They had a lot of loyal customers, but they were afraid they wouldn't make enough money to stay in business.

The advice given was in the form of specific questions:

◆ How much money do you need to make?

- What are your expenses?
- How many do you need to sell per year to cover all your expenses and leave you with a profit?
- How many is that per week?
- What do you need to do in order to sell that many each week?

They hadn't thought about it that way. They were just going to do the best they could. Were they unusual? No. That's the naive approach you want to avoid regardless of your industry.

OPPORTUNITIES IN SALES

There are tremendous opportunities in sales: opportunities for self-development, opportunities for promotion, opportunities for helping people, job satisfaction, financial wealth, and even progression towards running your own business if that's what you want. Yet, few business owners today succeed without strong emphasis and skills on the sales side. And likewise, few people today in the corporate world progress without being able to sell their ideas.

Millions of people are involved in the production of products or services. All of their jobs rely on people being able to sell those products or services. Corporations need you. The economies of the world rely on continued sales. Your skills and your success are more important than you realize.

MEASURE YOUR RESULTS

Whatever your goal, start now by measuring your targets and breaking them into daily targets and tasks. Remember that today is your day of preparation, and your success later will mainly depend on your plan and your dedication to your plan.

Two aspects on this chart are the most critical to measure:

◆ Number of sales visits (target and actual)

◆ Number of sales (target and actual)

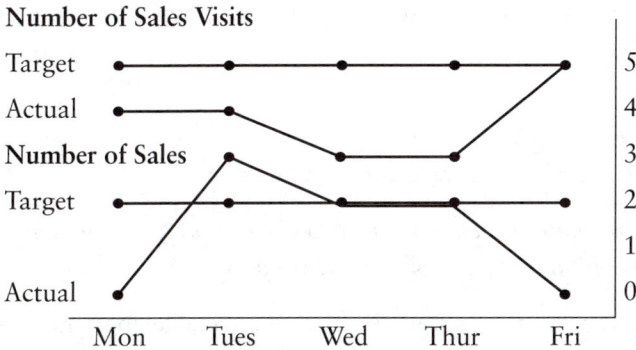

If you are really determined to succeed, you should also chart the following:

Self-Management systems

◆ The number of telephone calls you make for appointments (target and actual)

◆ The number of direct mail letters you send (target and actual)

◆ The number of referral leads you get from customers before and after the sale (target and actual)

◆ Any other methods you use for finding prospective customers

These will become your self-management systems.

PREDICTING SHORTFALLS

If your wall chart shows you that your actual sales visits are 25 percent below your target for one week, you can expect to be 25 percent down on sales unless you make up that number of visits next week.

Sales do not come about magically, and that's what your management control wall charts remind you of so graphically and unmistakably.

MENTAL READINESS

Will you reach the success level you hope for?

Much of your success will depend on coming to terms with the actual component parts of salesmanship.

Selling is not a mystical process. It's a predictable, logical, step-by-step process like a production line. When you put in the right component parts, you get the correct end-product. When you put in fewer component parts than necessary, you get an inferior end-product. There is no mystery about salesmanship.

Planning your success by setting your daily workload is the first component part. The next six chapters give the other component parts. When you carry out each component part in the right quantity, with the right quality and frequency, you have success.

Your results come from your actions, not from your understanding. It's said that, "Knowledge without action serves no one." This is never more true than in sales. Pick up your pen and start now to create your targets *and* your self-management system charts. Success is in your hands.

*Remember, knowledge without action
serves no one.*

Chapter 2

Gaining Product and Service Expertise

The purpose of this chapter is to help you create a personal plan for developing expertise in product and service knowledge that will help you reach the top of your profession.

You should realize that the activities described in this chapter, training and product/service research, may require significant amounts of time, sometimes weeks or months. Of course, although some of the training may take place before your selling career is under way, your development of product/service expertise continues during your entire sales career.

HOW MUCH EXPERTISE?

Let's start at the beginning. How much knowledge do you need? Perhaps this idea will help you. Dale Carnegie advised his students of public speaking, "Learn 40 times as much as you will use."

Why 40 times? It's because our store of information is like a fully charged battery. It shows in our enthusiasm, our self-confidence, and most of all in our *competence*. Certainly that's true of selling too.

Let's stop for a moment and think of your customers. How do they view you? Aren't you the only link between the manufactured product or service and themselves? They have to rely on you to tell them *each and every thing* that they might need to know.

◆ Gaining Product and Service Expertise

It makes sense, then, to have a 40-fold store of knowledge in reserve for every eventuality, over and above what we might use in a single sales discussion with a single customer. Therefore, you need to focus on getting as much knowledge as you can, as quickly as possible.

WHO IS RESPONSIBLE?

First, let's set the ground rules and clear any misconceptions. In order to reach the top with the desired level of expertise, you should consider these two principles:

◆ Expect to invest in yourself

◆ Don't expect the company to provide all of your training

INVEST IN YOURSELF

How many years do doctors, lawyers, or accountants spend in preparing themselves for their profession? If you want to become an expert, the first realization you must make is that you must invest in yourself. You have to develop your own plan. If your company trains you, fine. But you cannot use the lack of training as an excuse to hold you back. Success is in your own hands.

FINDING SOURCES OF KNOWLEDGE

Where do you start? You need to set a schedule for absorbing your 40-fold expertise in the shortest possible time. Let's look at some effective options.

Sources of product expertise

- Interview current customers
- Study product literature
- Study service literature
- Study operations manuals
- Take technicians on sales visits
- Accompany other sales professionals on sales visits
- Have discussions
  — with operations people
  — with managers
  — with product development people
  — with distributors
- Observe the production line
- Observe field service
- Take training courses of all kinds

♦ Gaining Product and Service Expertise

INTERVIEW CURRENT CUSTOMERS

Interviewing current customers is one of the most valuable yet least exploited options for salespeople. Customers give us the information from the *user's* point of view, which is invaluable.

GAIN BENEFITS

The customer doesn't want to know that the fax machine has "group 3, high speed, digital transmission technology." They only want to know that their document can reach their colleague in Australia in 28 seconds *because* of this group 3, high speed technology.

You must always stress the benefit of using the technology as proof that the benefit exists.

Why else are we so bullish on visiting or talking to current customers? Because they are a bottomless pit of testimonials, references, new business, add-on business, referrals, inspiration, enthusiasm, and information about competitors. Moreover, they can supply quotable stories, even material for press releases and feature stories. But the most important part is your instant education.

Here is an example. Some years ago I was involved in selling a computer service. Because all of us on the sales team were hired from industry and knew little about computers, we each needed to get our own training as quickly as possible. I therefore arranged to accompany a technician on a trouble-shooting call, and after she sorted out the problem, I asked the client a question: "What made you choose our system over the competitor's?"

"It's so fast to use and error free," he said. "We previously agonized over errors in our systems. Now we complete input forms every morning. It takes half an hour maximum. Then the results come back—perfect, no aggravation," he said.

That was a testimonial I could use to emphasize speed and accuracy. It gave our sales team a valuable reference letter and later we turned it into a press release, which gave it added value.

So you can see that the benefits of interviews with current customers are endless. Through interviews you gain confidence in your product and company. You learn the benefits to the user. You build a rapport that can later lead to further business. You acquire testimonial stories about how the service is used. You gain confidence and inspiration.

You can then repeat the process with different industry group users until you have the knowledge you need. The time it takes you will be well worth your while.

PLAN YOUR STRATEGY

Use today to plan your strategy for building your product/service expertise. The checklist below will help you decide which methods to apply. Who will you go to in order to get the information? How

♦ Gaining Product and Service Expertise

long will you allocate to each method? When will you do it? Use this list to create your action strategy.

Set up your system today. You may want to call one or two current customers to set up appointments for interviews. Or you may even want to have the discussion by telephone today if appropriate. Naturally, it's always better to do it in person if possible. Distances, time, and products will dictate the appropriate approach.

Look again at your strategy. Have you allocated enough time?

Product/service expertise

Method	Yes/No	Who	How Long	When
◆ Interview current customers	_____	_____	_____	_____
◆ Study product literature	_____	_____	_____	_____
◆ Study service literature	_____	_____	_____	_____
◆ Study operations manuals	_____	_____	_____	_____
◆ Take technicians on sales visits	_____	_____	_____	_____
◆ Accompany other sales professionals on sales visits	_____	_____	_____	_____

Method	Yes/No	Who	How Long	When

◆ Have discussions
   — with operations people　_____　_____　_____　_____
   — with managers　_____　_____　_____　_____
   — with product development people　_____　_____　_____　_____
   — with distributors　_____　_____　_____　_____

◆ Observe the production line　_____　_____　_____　_____

◆ Observe field service　_____　_____　_____　_____

◆ Take training courses　_____　_____　_____　_____

You may want to spend an hour a day next week reading technical literature or perhaps two hours today. You may want to invite a technical person to accompany you on your next sales visit, or arrange to accompany them on a technical visit. Decide now and allocate time in your schedule.

ATTEND TRAINING COURSES

You may want to persuade your manager that he or she should fund a training course for you from their budget. If you do, you should be prepared to "sell" your idea—explain the benefits the company will get from your enhanced skills. Remember, your boss may have to sell the idea up the line.

But beware of the bottom line—that is, your commitment to your own training. If the answer is no, you may have to invest in yourself. Be prepared to take responsibility for your own success.

Professionals spend time and money preparing for success in their career, and selling is as demanding and challenging as any career.

What steps can you take to find training courses that will be valuable to you?

LEARN AT EVERY APPOINTMENT

One top sales manager I knew summed it up well when he advised, "The day you stop learning in sales is the day your professionalism dies."

After every sales call with any of his sales staff, whether they were new to sales or experienced, he always said, "Tell me two new things you learned from that visit." That's good advice for all of us.

IMPLEMENT YOUR STRATEGY

Take time now to look back over the options for developing product and service expertise. Decide which options are right for you.

Then draw up a segmented strategy of how much time to devote to each option. Take today to plan those segments.

> *Remember, the day you stop learning is the day your professionalism dies.*

Chapter 3

Discover the Buying Motives

One university professor I know shocks his class by saying, "No one makes any decision in life that doesn't benefit himself in some way."

The students always protest, "Surely that's not true. People often do things for humanitarian reasons. There are church groups. There are people who do things unselfishly."

"Yes," the professor counters, "that's true. But let's look under the surface. What motivates them? What makes them make their decision? What do *they* get out of it?"

Then he goes on to explain that even in humanitarian actions, people feel good about themselves and their noble actions. This is a benefit to them.

MOTIVES CAN BE PSYCHOLOGICAL

Gradually the students learn to examine the motives behind decisions and to look for what drives people. They discover that the benefits people get can be psychological as well as material.

Think of this as it relates to your own sales situation. What benefits do your customers get? Don't think about what the product does. Think about the benefit to the buyer.

◆ Discover the Buying Motives

THE CORRECT WAY TO FIND MOTIVES

Perhaps you've heard this saying. "The person who asks the questions is in control of the meeting."

In order to be in control of your success, it's necessary to ask questions. Not just any questions. They must be questions that lead to the customer's needs and buying motives.

One time I sat with a new employee and discussed a prospective client. I told the employee that it would be his job at the upcoming meeting to ask questions that would lead us to the buying motive of the client. He said he could do it because he considered himself to be a good conversationalist.

After 45 minutes with the customer it was obvious that my employee was taking the conversation in all directions *except* to discover why he might want our service. The employee hadn't learned to *target* his conversation in a certain direction. It was a hit and miss approach.

Hit and miss doesn't work in selling because we don't have the time we have in social relationships. We have to ask precise questions that lead us in the direction of the answers we need in order to identify our clients' needs, and then stress the corresponding benefits.

Let's look at some possible questions:

◆ What do you expect from a supplier?

◆ What benefit are you hoping for?

◆ What one thing could we offer to convince you to change suppliers?

◆ What can we do as a supplier to help you achieve your goals?

◆ How can we fit into your plans as a member of your team?

Those are five precise and very directive questions. They lead you in the direction of finding out the needs and motives of your client. Now think of more questions. Create your own list.

Think of yourself as a yachtsman with the rudder of your sailboat in the grip of your hand. As your boat goes slightly off course, you move the rudder to bring it back on course.

To become a powerful and directive questioner you need only think of yourself as a yachtsman. When the conversation starts to go off course, when it starts to wander aimlessly in this direction or that, you need to bring it back on course. "Yes, I see what you mean. That's important to know. I remember you said earlier that you wanted a high clarity screen . . . ," and so you are back on track. "What benefits are you looking for—higher productivity, faster turnaround, less frustration?" you continue.

Practice, practice, practice bringing the conversation back to ascertaining the customer's needs and motives. The person who asks the questions sets the direction. You must make sure you know what direction you want to go in.

GET THE LOGICAL AND PSYCHOLOGICAL MOTIVES

You can actually help our buyer on two levels: the logical level and the psychological level.

Another way to look at this is to say that every corporate purchase has a benefit to the corporation and a benefit to the individual. Most salespeople focus only on the logical or corporate benefit. Yet the psychological or individual benefit can be, and often is, far more powerful and persuasive.

Why not go away to a quiet place and list your prospects. What are their emotional or individual buying motives?

◆ *What do they need and want?*

◆ *What benefits can I match to their needs?*

CHECK YOUR ASSUMPTIONS

The title of this chapter is "*Discover* the Buying Motives." Yet sales are lost because people *assume* they know what the customer wants.

Successful Selling

Checklist of assumptions about needs and buying motives

List the assumptions you and your colleagues may be making about the needs and buying motives of your prospects:

- Price (too high). Why?
- Price (too low). Why?
- Extras (important). Why?
- Extras (not important). Why?
- Distance
- Delivery time
- Features
- Benefits
- Service

List all the assumptions you can think of. Examine them and ask why you have this assumption. Is it something this customer said? Is it something ingrained from the last customer? Is it something your colleague said about the customer? Does it need to be validated?

The best method of checking your assumptions is to call your customers and ask if your assumptions are right. Then you must *listen* to their answers and reshape your presentation or proposal accordingly. If it's a team sell, you need to convince your colleagues to avoid these costly assumptions also.

Thus you realize how much time and effort you've lost barking up the wrong tree, and change your approach to selling. If you really want to excel in avoiding assumptions, track the reasons for every sale you lose or have lost. The best companies do just that.

In *Secrets of the World's Top Sales Performers*, Sony employees told us that they sit together and examine their approach and assumptions. They don't point fingers in order to place the blame outside; rather they decide what caused the loss and how to overcome it next time.

During your analyses, you'll discover that your assumptions on buying motives are fatal. It's a fast cure and a lesson every professional needs to learn.

DECISION MAKERS' ASSUMPTIONS TO AVOID

When calling to find out why the business was lost, you'll discover that there were pressures within the organization that eluded you.

One seminar delegate I met told the story of working closely for several months with the managing director of a company to identify his needs. He thought everything was perfect until he presented the final proposal and discovered that the production director also had influence.

What did he do wrong? His error is common and painful. He assumed that the MD's authority was enough. He didn't identify the people who influenced the purchase decision and therefore didn't find out their needs.

THE TIME TO PRESENT MOTIVES

One computer systems saleswoman in America is constantly ranked at the top of her national sales team. Janet achieves 190 percent of her target year after year.

Successful Selling

Let's look at the critical difference between Janet's approach, which keeps her at the top end, and the approach of salespeople who are average in performance.

She has an invaluable two-tier approach. She visits the prospective client on a fact-finding mission, and interviews them thoroughly to ascertain their needs and motives. She also makes sure she interviews everyone who influences the buying decision.

Only then does she present the benefit of her product and in such a way that it precisely meets the customer's needs.

She focuses all her energy and all her words on what the customer will gain from the system. Her preparation time goes into thinking about how the system can match the needs of each individual and therefore justify the costs in their minds.

The average salesperson doesn't hit the bull's-eye because their questioning process fails them. Their needs analysis and motive analysis are missing or inadequate. They do not sell as often as they could. Let's look at the vital rules:

◆ Discover the Buying Motives

- ◆ Never assume you know the customer's needs and motives.
- ◆ Identify all individuals who influence the purchase decision.
- ◆ Interview to uncover needs and motives.
- ◆ Get their logical and psychological motives.
- ◆ Go away and think.
- ◆ Express the product or service benefits that match the customer's needs and motives.
- ◆ Only then present to the customer with complete focus on *their* buying motives.

PRESENT MOTIVES LINKED TO BENEFITS

During the time you think before your presentation, you will have made notes, listed those who influence the decision, thought about everyone's needs. You will have looked at the presentation from all sides, like a three-dimensional picture. You'll have thought about all angles in preparation for your next approach to them.

Making a grid like the one shown here will help you see clearly what actions need to be taken next. On the horizontal scale list the benefits of your product (for example, A—where A is quality, B—where B is price, C—where C is performance, D—where D is reliability, E—where E is service, F—where F is suitability to customer need, or whatever your benefits are). On the vertical scale list the needs of each company for each benefit listed on the horizontal scale.

Our Product Benefits		A	B	C	D	E	F
Needs of Company X	1.						
	2.						
	3.						
	4.						
Needs of Company Y	1.						
	2.						
	3.						
	4.						
Psychological needs of Customer A	1.						
	2.						
	3.						
	4.						
Psychological needs of Customer B	1.						
	2.						
	3.						
	4.						

◆ Discover the Buying Motives

READY, SET, GO

Armed with your list of buying motives and the benefits you can offer to meet their needs, you have nothing to fear.

Now you see clearly what to present. When you go to your customer, you will not be "winging it." You will not be improvising. You will be presenting our product or service in such a way that they can see the benefit and justify it. Their logical and emotional needs will be met. It will all fall into place.

Why? Because the customer's buying motive has had the preeminent position. You will have stepped into the customer's shoes and seen it from their point of view. You will be on their side of the fence and they will feel it.

Remember, the person who asks the questions guides the direction. Make sure you steer in the direction of the buying motives.

Chapter 4

Overcome Objections

When you are handling objections, whether in selling or in everyday life, you're dealing with very human factors. You're dealing with people's need to be heard—people's need to be recognized for their opinions, fears, doubts, and misunderstandings.

This takes finesse on your part. It takes time to stop and think. It takes determination to do things a new way.

Let's look at two examples in which we can apply the objections process to improve our results. Some years ago I gave a speech to 150 people from a political party that had previously taken our sales and marketing course.

After my speech I asked some of them, "What did you implement from the course so far?" Their immediate answer was, "Better ways of handling the objections of our electorate." Thus you can see the importance of being able to sell and defend your ideas. The same is true in the workplace and in all areas of life.

Here is a personal example of the power of the objection process. After learning this process, one of our instructors reported that he had tremendously improved his relationship with his teenage daughter. "How did it happen?" I asked.

"I applied the three-part objection technique we teach in class," he reported. His daughter told him that it was the first time she felt he had really listened to her. Thus her attitude and cooperation improved enormously.

In selling, if you don't clear the objection, it lingers like smoke in the mind of our customers. You must clear it just as you clear smoke from a room. Think of a large fan blowing the smoke out through an open window. That's what you're doing with the objection-clearing process.

THE PROCESS

The three-part process can have extraordinary results for you too. Here are the steps:

- The preamble (psychological)
- The explanation (logical)
- The clarification question (psychological)

THE PREAMBLE

Your preamble segment prepares people to listen by melting down their defenses. Do this by making it clear that you do consider the other sides of the issue. Encourage a full explanation of those concerns. Ask questions. Express your understanding.

Most people put the spotlight on the explanation. They forget that the explanation falls on deaf ears if they don't break down the defenses of the customer first. When I refer to the "customer" in this case, of course I'm referring to your listener, be it your boss, your spouse, your child, your political constituents, your colleague, or your client.

If the customer says no, then we have to have further discussion. But chances are that he won't, because your words have made him feel that you understand his concerns. You didn't ride roughshod over his objections. You took time to sympathize, to get on his side, to see his point of view first, before you brought out your logical explanation.

The preamble gives the other person a chance

◆ to cool down.

◆ to realize you're on his side.

◆ to feel understood.

◆ to have his concerns validated.

- to save face.
- to build a rapport with you.

◆

The key point to understand here is this: No matter how good your explanation segment, it won't sink in until you convince people that you sympathize with and value their concerns.

HANDLING PRICE OBJECTIONS

Let's look at a hot subject with salespeople—overcoming the price objection. First let's look at the difference between success and failure. The truth is that most ineffective salespeople *think* that they could sell *if* their price was lower.

Yet, most top salespeople don't consider price to be an obstacle. Why? Think about this because chances are that you've fallen into the same trap from time to time.

Why do the top performers breeze past the price objections when others are blocked?

The reasons are *attitude* and *understanding*. If you think your price is too high, you can be sure you'll transmit that to your customer. If you think your price is too high, you won't look for the benefits that justify the price.

Would your company really stay in business if the price didn't justify the benefits? Probably not.

If the price really is too high, then it's time to cure the problem or change jobs. The point is this: *don't* make the mistake of the majority of ineffective salespeople, which is to try and ignore price justifications.

You must get out there and *learn* price justifications as the top performers do. That will form your logical explanation segment. And you must remember to have a preamble discussion before you commence your price justification.

Why not put the technique into practice and see what you can achieve? I think you'll be surprised. You can work on your answers today by using the chart on page 41 and the example that follows.

EXAMPLE

"I like your product, but the price is too high," your customer says. At this point you don't know what he means by "too high." Higher than the competition for exactly the same thing, higher than his budget, higher than his expectation? But you can't ask yet because you haven't broken down the resistance.

Think about what your preamble should be. It must be right for you and your customer. Fill the appropriate response into the chart on page 41, perhaps something like this:

"Yes, I can understand your concern about price, Miss Whitehill. With the economy the way it is, businesses have to make every penny count. In fact, you're not alone. A lot of our clients told us they were worried about price before they used our service. Yet afterwards they come back and tell us they had a 100 percent payback within three weeks."

THE EXPLANATION

Now you're making your transition to the logical explanation. In your preamble you sympathized with *the customer's* concern. You even said others felt the same.

You're going out of your way to prove you understand the concern from the customer's point of view.

Now, what *are* your price justification benefits? What reasons do you have that will justify the expenditure? Chances are that you'll find dozens when you start digging.

You'll be most effective if you get these from current and past customers, because you'll have high credibility stories to tell your clients.

Successful Selling

For example, "Mr. Phillips at Tarmaco told me last week that they reduced their down time by 30 minutes per day with our service. This amounted to a savings of $10,000 per year."

You should always match the customer's buying motives to the benefits you put forward. You shouldn't talk about down time if it's irrelevant. Choose some benefit that does justify the price to that particular customer.

BRAINSTORM PRICE JUSTIFICATION

Look again at the objection chart on page 41 and list all the price justifications you can think of, then talk to colleagues and customers to expand the list.

Start your list now before you read on. Even if it's just one or two points scribbled on a scrap of paper, it will get you started. The first step is the hardest, but you must take it if you want to get on the winning path.

Remember, success is in your actions, not your realizations. You must be unrelenting with yourself when you're forming new habits of success.

CLARIFICATION QUESTION

Now it's time for your clarification question. "Have I satisfied your concerns on the price, Miss Whitehill?"

"Well, yes but I'm still concerned about the set-up cost," she responds.

Good. Now you realize she's satisfied about the running costs, but she has a concern about the set-up costs. That's not a problem.

◆ Overcome Objections

Use the three-part process again.

◆ Start at the beginning with another preamble.

◆ Then go to the second step, the logical explanation. Give the benefits she'll receive in exchange for the price she pays for set-up.

◆ Then go to the third step. Ask a question to see if she accepts your explanation.

Three-part objection process chart

1. Preamble (human/psychological factor)
This opens the iron gate and breaks down the resistance.

2. Explanation (logical factor)
Justification—benefits received in exchange for money paid out.

a.

b.

c.

d.

3. Clarification Question (human/psychological factor)
Does your customer understand and accept your explanation?

CLOSING DESPITE OBJECTIONS

You may never satisfy every concern a customer has. There will always be a competitor who offers something you don't offer. There will always be requests you can't fulfill. But when you can satisfy enough concerns to outweigh the doubts, you will succeed.

You can always use the direct approach: "Miss Whitehill, we've discussed a checklist of ten requirements you hoped to meet. We couldn't meet two, but we *could* meet eight. I hope that the ones we can meet are the significant ones. I see those eight as being . . ." (You list the benefits and price justifications that relate to her.)

You ask, "Does it sound like the kind of service you would benefit from?" *Thus you help the customer put the situation into perspective*. Chances are that eight out of ten of the requirements are enough to meet their demands, especially if the requirements you can offer outweigh the ones you can't offer.

◆ Overcome Objections

BE ARMED AHEAD

In preparation for your success ahead, you should be armed with a list of likely objections and responses. Use the following chart and add as many sheets as you need to be prepared for most eventualities.

The answers that you prepare ahead on this chart can be used during sales presentations, telephone calls with prospective customers, and even in written communication.

Think now about all the areas in which you can use the three-part objection clearing process. Set a target today for improving your success rate in overcoming objections.

Now think of ways to:

◆ Practice it

◆ Remember to do it

Remember, the preamble is the key to having your explanation accepted. It breaks down the iron gate of resistance.

Objection reference chart

1. Price
  Preamble statement
  Explanation statement
  Satisfaction/question

2. Delivery Time
  Preamble statement
  Explanation statement
  Satisfaction/question

3. Lack of expertise
  Preamble statement
  Explanation statement
  Satisfaction/question

List any other likely objections:

4. _____

  Preamble statement
  Explanation statement
  Satisfaction/question

5. _____

  Preamble statement
  Explanation statement
  Satisfaction/question

6. _____

  Preamble statement
  Explanation statement
  Satisfaction/question

Chapter 5

Presentations and Closings

In your sales presentation, when you combine the facts with the answers to the following questions, you'll be able to make critical links. These links will be the green light to your sale.

ASK QUESTIONS TO DETERMINE THE CUSTOMER'S CORPORATE BUYING MOTIVE

Let's consider the few facts about why most people buy your product or service, even though there are no specific facts about why *this* customer wants your product.

Assumptions don't count in sales, but as you ask questions more and more facts will help you to link the buying motive to the benefits you have to offer. The difference between you, a top sales performer, and a mediocre sales performer is that you will ask and ask until you have all the facts and answers. You'll find out the buying motives of every decision maker and every decision influencer. Each answer, each fact, will add more knowledge to your personal store.

The mediocre sales performers will not take time to ask because they assume that this customer is like all the others. These false assumptions will lead them to impure links. The benefits they offer to the client will therefore be right for other customers but not necessarily right for this customer. Their time will be spent in vain. You won't let this happen to you because you realize that the time spent here is the most valuable of all.

ASK QUESTIONS TO DETERMINE THE CUSTOMER'S PERSONAL BUYING MOTIVE

Most ineffective salespeople don't even look for the customer's personal buying motive. They assume that the corporate buying motive is all important. Yes, of course, you can't sell without satisfying the corporate buying motive, but you must not discount one important factor: **How will you get your buyer to fight personally for the sale?**

If your customer contact in the corporate ladder is not personally motivated, why should she bother? After all, she has a job to do. Your sales efforts are an intrusion in her busy schedule.

You must identify what's in it for your customer personally. Is it

- saving time?
- improving prestige?
- reducing chaos?
- reducing stress?
- improving morale?
- being up to date?
- career advancement?
- more free time?

What is it that can motivate her personally? You have to *ask*. You have to find genuine answers and facts in order to create the genuine links necessary to sell.

KNOW YOUR PRODUCT AS AN EXPERT

As you are turning their situation around and around in your mind, the links are building up faster and faster. You *know* all the facts about your product and service—you're an expert in it. Now you are learning the answers to all your questions about the customer's corporate and personal buying motives. All of these are merging in your mind—the combination of needs and benefits that is the reason people will buy.

You've painstakingly talked to current customers to find out why they use your products. You've found out what benefits they get. You *know* what you have to offer to prospective customers in every detail. You've consulted your literature and your internal experts. You *know*.

KNOW THE COMPETITION'S STRENGTH AND WEAKNESS

Don't be afraid of the competition. Knowledge is power. The more you know, the better position you will be in to defend the benefits *you* can offer. Your competitor may have some marvelous features, but if those features are not important to your client, you can still sell your benefits and win.

The important thing is to be informed about what the competition *does* offer. Then you won't be taken by surprise. Then you'll have time to turn it around in your mind, to become comfortable with it in a matter of fact way, to accept it as a feature, but put it in perspective.

"Yes," you can say to yourself, "they have this feature, we have that. Now let's see who needs what. Let's look at the combination of benefits. Let's look at the cost of their benefits and of our benefits, and find out who is willing to pay what for those benefits."

Then when a customer says that your competitor has feature "A," you'll be able to say, "Yes, how do you feel about that feature?

◆ Presentations and Closings

There are many features in the marketplace today. We've created ours by researching what our users most wanted for the price, ease of use," etc. You then help the customer put it into perspective.

By helping them reevaluate it, they may see that it's not important at all. The last salesperson may have made them feel they couldn't live without this special feature. But you, through your thoroughness of asking about their buying motives, can help them reflect on specific issues.

◆ Do they really need this?

◆ Is it really an advantage?

◆ Will they really use it, or is there a down side?

◆ What will it cost the customer either financially or in terms of learning time and energy?

◆ What will they have to give up in order to gain that?

◆ What are the start-up and continuation costs?

◆ What does your package of features and benefits have to offer over theirs?

Knowledge is power. Because you know a lot about the competitors, you're in a position of strength, not weakness. You have little to fear. You'll be able to make links that work for you *and* the client.

TELL ABOUT THE LINKS BETWEEN THEIR NEED AND YOUR BENEFITS

This is the moment of truth—literally. If you have the truth in terms of the buyer's needs and motives, if you have all the facts about what your products can do, then you'll be able to make the links that give the buyer the mental green light to buy.

Successful Selling

Selling today is not a manipulative process. Selling is helping the customer *see* what you have to offer and *how* it meets their needs. Notice that there are two parts to this and the second part is the key to success.

◆ What you have to offer

◆ How it meets their needs

Many ineffective salespeople focus on only the first part. They don't stop to realize that a customer doesn't want to buy from someone who says, "We can do this, *we* can do this, *we* can do this."

Who is the most important person in the world? The customer, of course. Will he feel important or feel cared about with a salesperson who talks only about his product and what it can do? Of course not. It's the *link* that makes the sale.

And you can't make the link without asking the customer what he wants, what benefit he sees, what his objective is, how he will use it. You don't do it as an interrogation, but rather from a position of consultative concern, of really trying to help.

Don't make the mistake of the ineffective salesperson, doing only half the job. You'll get only half the results. Do the whole job—make the link. Tell the customer how the product meets his needs. Do this and your sales will more than double. This is true in every industry from retail to aerospace, from products and services to politics and education. If you want to sell anything, even an idea, you have to make a *flawless* link of the needs of the customer with the benefits they will get.

Make a list now of benefits and the likely motives of several prospective customers you'll see. This process will help you to think on your feet when you see them.

◆ Presentations and Closings

For example:

Needs-Benefit Link Chart

Need Customer wants to reduce overheads in the department next year by $25,000.

Benefit System saves 20 percent man hours over his current system.

Link Customer will be able to do without two members of staff, saving $50,000. This $50,000 in overhead reduction will pay for the system the first year as well as reduce his running costs by $25,000, which was his goal. From then on the customer continues to save every year.

1. Customer B
   Need:
   Benefit:
   Link:

2. Customer C
   Need:
   Benefit:
   Link:

3. Customer D
   Need:
   Benefit:
   Link:

◆

After this link-building expertise is developed, you'll be able to communicate it verbally or in writing or both, thus increasing your closing rate.

TELL HOW YOU OVERCOME OBJECTIONS

Remember that objections linger like smoke. However, *you* won't let your customer's objections linger because you'll use the three-part objection technique from page 41. You'll make them realize that you *do* sympathize, you *do* understand. Then you'll give the explanation, and then you'll check to see if their concern is satisfied.

Ineffective salespeople do not see the value in this. They don't want to be involved in this sort of activity. It makes them uncomfortable. They want to sweep any hint of objection under the rug, hoping naively that it will never resurface. Little do they know that it smolders there while the customer's mind becomes locked into the idea that her objection is reality. The customer is mentally packing her briefcase to go home while the ineffective salesperson continues to talk—*unheard*.

◆ Presentations and Closings

You, however, have the facts and the answers. Therefore, you counter their objections quickly and easily as if holding the hand of the customer and walking them through a maze. You can do this because you've studied the likely objections and solutions and you've asked questions to find out what the customer's concerns are.

REVIEW NEEDS AND BENEFITS

This is the most rewarding because it reveals the big picture. It puts everything into perspective for the customer. You've discussed features, benefits, needs, motives, and objections. Now you are ready for the big picture.

"You told me you wanted to achieve X, Y, and Z. Is this still the case?" you must ask. You're helping them refocus on their needs, cut out the extraneous, forget the glorified benefits offered by the competitors.

Next you say, "We've looked at our ability to meet X, Y, and Z through these methods . . ." You express the benefits of your product succinctly. You don't elaborate so long that the customer forgets what X, Y, and Z are.

Keep your choice of words focused on what they get, not what you give. "With this machine you can get your documents to your office in Australia in 28 seconds. This will help you meet your objective of speeding up your communication time in order to win contracts."

You won't say, "This machine gives you group 3, high speed, digital transmission technology." That's about the machine, not the customer. In addition, it doesn't mention her objective at all.

Yet that's how most uninitiated salespeople handle their presentation. Not you, of course, because you've done your homework and combined the customer's needs with your benefits. You've sifted through the important versus the unimportant benefits to the customer, and you have stressed the important ones.

Next you approach the most vital element in your task.

ASK FOR THEIR DECISION

Recent research has shown that four out of five buyers *expect* to be asked to buy and *wait* to be asked. They don't volunteer to buy because they expect us, as part of the selling process, to ask. They wait, and if it doesn't happen, the buying moment passes by.

Let's look at what causes the critical moment to pass. Several things could happen. A competitor could ask for the order and get it, the customer could lose interest, or he could divert the funds to another project. Therefore, the ineffective person who doesn't ask, loses.

But your approach is different. From the beginning you have been thorough. You've been letting the customer know how your product or service can help him, thus building commitment each step of the way. Your approach has let him see himself using and benefiting from the product. Now when you ask for his decision, it's almost a foregone conclusion. The benefits are crystal clear and they *line up exactly* with the customer's expressed needs.

You've been a catalyst in the customer's search for the answer. You've helped him make his way through the maze of the unknown. You've helped him see the solution. Now when you ask for his decision, it's not an abrupt surprise. It's not a pressured, stressful event. It's a natural evolution and the customer expects questions.

- "Do you wish to purchase this?" you might ask at the retail counter.
- "Do you think this is the kind of service that would benefit you?" you might ask in the sale of services.
- "Are the advantages we offer more meaningful than the other suppliers?" we might ask in system sales.
- "Would you like to work with us on this project?"
- "What implementation schedule should we meet?"

Stop now and make a list of closing questions that feel right for you. Then when you get to this stage of your presentation, you won't have anything to fear. You'll have question after question that you designed and that work for *you*, not someone else.

Do you know the secret of success over others who fail? They have only a little bit of product knowledge. They ask no questions to ascertain needs (they assume they know). They make no links to needs. They talk about the product only. They avoid objections whenever possible. And they don't ask for the business.

In your case it is different. You are building your own professionalism, which makes you a desirable commodity. Keep it up. The rewards are coming your way.

> *Remember, four out of five customers*
> *wait for us to ask for the order.*
> *Don't just make a presentation.*
> *Make a presentation* and *ask for the business.*

Chapter 6

Action-Provoking Systems

Striking while the iron is hot is a critical issue.

If you follow up a direct mail letter by telephone two weeks after it's sent, your call will be one-fifth as effective as it would be if you called after three days.

Why? Because people forget 80 percent of what they hear and read after two days. If you call shortly after the letter is posted, it will be fresh in their minds. If you call after three weeks, it won't.

Customer Interest Cycle

Peak buying period

80% of salespeople put their peak effort here, causing them to be ineffective

| Gaining interest period | Maximum interest period | Losing interest period |

The same is true of following up your prospect for a decision. What's the point of following up too late—after your competitor goes in or after your customer's budget is diverted?

WORK HARD OR WORK INTELLIGENTLY?
The fact is that the majority of salespeople put their time and effort into the sales process too late. Because they don't have action-provoking systems, they do things when they have time. Often this is too late.

BENEFITS OF ACTION-PROVOKING SYSTEMS
An action-provoking system will help you use your time where it counts—closing sales you have already started and starting the correct number of new prospects necessary to meet your targets.

WHAT'S YOUR EXPERIENCE?
What kind of system do you have now?

Perhaps your experience is something like John's, an experienced salesman who came to our course. He was looking desperately for a way to increase his sales, but didn't know which way to turn.

We asked him what sort of action-provoking system he had and he said he wrote everything in his diary.

He said he carried everything over to the new page. Yet he admitted it was a lot of work to carry it forward and easy to miss or forget some. We looked at John's system and showed him this chart.

Successful Selling

Action-Provoking System

June	1	2	3	4	5	6	7
1. Smith & Co	X						
2. J Bloggs							
3. Estman		X					
4. Winters		X					
5. Peak and Co							
6. Johnston							
7. Withers							
8. Goodall & Co.		X					
9. Jones Bros							
10. Kent Air							
11. P.V. Anchor	X						
12. Bassett		X					

"The beauty of this system," we told him, "is that we can walk into our office in the morning and see at a glance all our prime prospects. We know immediately which ones need action.

"On June 1 two companies need action from us. On June 2, four companies need action. They are the ones on lines 3, 4, 8, and 12. We just pull out those files and see what action is necessary."

TWO CRITICAL ADVANTAGES

This system gives you two critical advantages. First, you're not likely to forget anyone. Their name is already entered. Secondly, you see at a glance much more about your prospect.

Let's say you call someone five days in a row and you miss them each time. We'll put an X down for the next consecutive day to remind you to call.

Later you'll have more critical information. You'll be able to glance at your sheet and see five X marks side by side. You'll know your efforts aren't succeeding. If this is a hot prospect, you'd better double up your efforts or take other action.

John looked skeptical but he went away and tried it. He called us a month later and said that the results of his new system put him up 40 percent on his sales figures after only 30 days.

WEAKNESS OF DIARY SYSTEMS

"The diary system used to let me lose prospects too conveniently," he told us. "I've closed three sales this month by entering them into the master system. I know I would have turned the page and forgotten them in my old diary system. But because they were on the master sheet, I couldn't forget. It also made me more aware of my hard work on each prospect to date by seeing all my actions on one sheet. It made me more determined. I felt more in control."

You may have the same reluctance that John had at first. You probably have a system that works for you. Fine. But the question is this:

◆ How well is it working?

◆ How much is slipping through the net that you're not aware of?

If you're looking for sales excellence, you have to turn over every stone of your present practices and see if there is a way of doing anything differently. You might find a way to make a small change in your practices that can get you enormously higher results.

Take today to examine your system and find the weak points or to develop a new system.

COMPUTERIZED SYSTEMS

FIND THE FALLACY

"We have a perfect computerized system," one salesman said. "It tells us everything we've done for a prospect and what stage it's at."

"Great," we said. "Does it tell you what day you have to take the next action? Does it show you on any given day a list of every prospect that needs action that day?"

"Well, I'm not sure," he said. "But we can pull up any prospect name and see the history of our actions."

Think about what he's just said and see if you can find two fallacies. There's nothing wrong with history, but history is history. It doesn't provoke us to action on a certain day. What we're looking for is an action-*provoking* system, not historical record-keeping.

So there we have the first fallacy—confusing "action taken" with action "to be taken." You want a report that lets you see a list of critical actions at the beginning of each day.

You also need a report that shows every company that should *have been* actioned in the past, with the number of days outstanding next to it like an aged debtors report that accountants use.

Only then do you have a good system. Only then do you know if you are striking while the "iron is hot."

Think again about the computer system of the salesman above and where you can see the second fallacy. When we asked him if he got a list of prospects that need action every day, he said he *wasn't sure*.

♦ Action-Provoking Systems

What does that tell us about his use of the system? It tells us he wasn't using it, at least not to help him prompt his daily actions.

There's no point in having systems we don't use, and it becomes even more dangerous to think we have systems that help us when in fact they don't.

Look at your systems cold and hard now and ask, "Are they really helping?" If not, don't fool yourself into thinking they are. Make something quick and easy that works for you.

MANUAL SYSTEMS FOR PROSPECTING

Here's a useful manual system if you have hundreds of prospects to deal with at once.

This system consists of two ring binder notebooks. It's especially useful for telesales and telephone appointments.

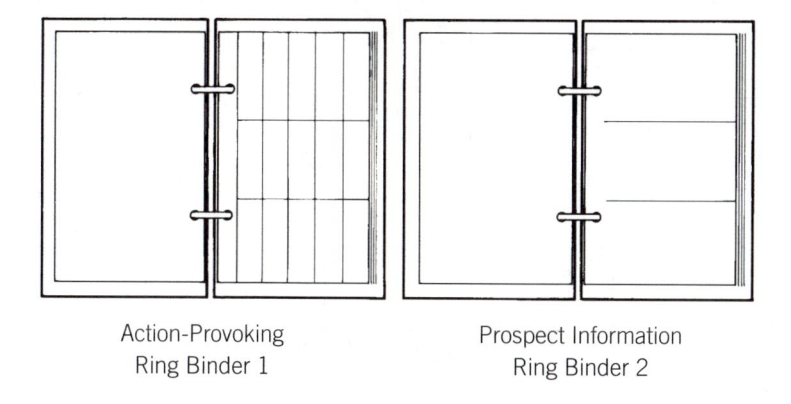

Action-Provoking
Ring Binder 1

Prospect Information
Ring Binder 2

In Ring Binder 1 are 52 sheets, each representing one week of the year. On each sheet there is a week number, date, and days of the week across the top.

Successful Selling

Down the side there is a place to list

- new prospects
- follow-up prospects
- appointment confirmations

Each sheet looks like this:

Action-Provoking Ring Binder 1			
◯ Week Number_____ Date_____			
New Prospects			
Mon	*Tues*	*Wed*	*Thurs*	*Fri*
◯ **Follow-up Prospects**			
Appointment Confirmations			
◯				

♦ Action-Provoking Systems

On Monday, you walk into the office knowing that *you must activate a certain number of new prospects*. This number depends on your yearly target, which we've broken down to a daily figure. Your prospects might come from a phone book or a chamber of commerce list, an industry list, or a list of direct mail letters already mailed.

Now you are ready to follow each up by telephone. You go to Prospect Information Ring Binder 2, which holds your prospect information.

Each sheet looks like this:

Prospect Information Ring Binder 2
○ Company Name　　　　　　　　　　Code Number *A-103* 　Person 　Title 　Address 　Phone/Fax/e-mail 　Contact Date and Discussion Details
Company Name　　　　　　　　　　Code Number *A-104* 　Person ○ Title 　Address 　Phone/Fax/e-mail 　Contact Date and Discussion Details
Company Name　　　　　　　　　　Code Number *A-105* 　Person 　Title 　Address 　Phone/Fax/e-mail ○ Contact Date and Discussion Details

Successful Selling

Three or more prospects can fit easily on one page. Because of the volume of prospects, you give each a code number, which is easier to fit onto one sheet in the action-provoking ring binder.

By Monday night your sheet will look like this:

Action-Provoking Ring Binder 1				
Week Number_____ Date_____				
New Prospects				
Mon *A 105* *A 106* *A 107* *A 108* *A 109* *A 110*	Tues *A 105* *A 109*	Wed	Thurs	Fri
Follow-up Prospects				
A 65 *A 22* *A 37* *A 88* *A 94*	*A 88*			
Appointment Confirmations				
A 80 *A 26* *A 34*	*A 80*			

♦ Action-Provoking Systems

You'll see that most prospects have been spoken to. These have diagonal lines through them. Prospects A105, 109, 88, and 80 have not been reached and therefore they are listed for action on Tuesday.

All records are kept in the prospect information Ring Binder 1, and when that is full Ring Binder 2 is created.

Instead of using a series of notebooks for prospect information, file cards and file boxes can be used. But the notebook system prevents you from losing and misplacing cards and is much more convenient to transport from desk to desk or office to car.

When you get enough detail on one prospect, you may choose to start a file on them in the filing cabinet.

Take time to think of what system will work for you. Ask yourself:

♦ Where will I be when I use the system (car, desk, other)?

♦ How many entries will I need per day or week or month?

♦ What size book or record sheets do I need?

♦ Where will I store back-up information?

♦ What should the system look like?

♦ Who will use it: I, others?

♦ Who will enter the prospect names?

♦ Who will enter the next actions required and the dates they must be done?

♦ What time of day will I take action, such as phone calls for appointments, phone calls for follow up?

♦ Other questions to suit your situation.

Without an action-provoking system, you don't have the support system you need. Your energy is fragmented and at the end of the month you're disappointed you didn't get the results you hoped for.

Take today to design an action-provoking system to make your efforts effective.

> *Remember, your action-provoking system puts you in control.*

Chapter 7

Self-Motivation and Support Systems

Successful Selling

"Everyone gets into the doldrums," my first sales manager told our sales team, "but it's up to each of you to get yourselves out of it."

It would be nice if we all had sales managers who could coach us and encourage us at every turn like the best football coach.

But that's not practical. Managers are occupied with many activities, and they can't possibly know our personality and motivational needs as well as we can. And most importantly, our success is reliant on whom—us or them?

BE YOUR OWN COACH

What's the message? You can't wait for someone else to motivate you and set up your motivation systems for you. You have to do it yourself. You have to carry your own football coach in your mind.

WHAT SUPPORT IS NEEDED?

Let's look at the kind of encouragement most salespeople need and want. Think about your own situation carefully. What kind of support do you want when you have a "down" day? What kind of support do you want on normal days? Be specific and complete the list for yourself.

- Goal setting
- Reaching a particular milestone
- Doing a mundane task consistently
- Cold calling
- Getting appointments
- Morale boost
- Confidence building

What motivation and support systems can you put into place that will allow you to reach the top?

In this chapter we'll study the self-motivation and support systems of the top achievers so that you can choose those that would work for you and put the systems into place today.

These success systems include:

- People
- Staying positive

- Eliminating doldrums
- Daring to be different
- Overcoming roadblocks
- Moving speedily towards your goal

PEOPLE

What do you need from people? One top salesman talks to his wife from his car phone four times a day. He likes having someone to share his progress with, his ups and downs, his trials and tribulations.

Decide what support you want from people. All of us have people in our lives willing to support us, especially if we're willing to support them.

Who do you have? Open your mind to an expanded group of potential supporters. Partners, friends, coworkers, sales manager, other managers, people from your social or religious groups, new age thinkers, the community, chambers of commerce, new acquaintances, customers.

♦ Self-Motivation and Support Systems

Be specific about the kind of support you want from your list at the beginning of the chapter. Then set your goals, and share your progress with your supporter. Just reporting your progress to someone every day for a week, for example, can start you on a new path or help you form a new habit. I do this with a friend of mine who also owns a company.

Think now. Who can you talk to? You'll be surprised at how many people there are who would like to have this support reciprocated.

STAYING POSITIVE

What are the chances that your customer will be positive if you aren't? The answer is zero.

We all have negative thoughts that pass through our minds, but it's our choice whether to hang on to them or not. The first step is to notice what our thoughts are.

NOTICE YOUR THOUGHTS

If you were to count the number of thoughts that flash through the mind in one minute, you would reach well over 60.

We can't hold onto every one, so why not pick the positive ones? So often in life we give in to the negative ones, forgetting that we are in charge of either holding onto or releasing those thoughts.

RELEASE THE NEGATIVE

One top sales executive I know has developed his own mind-clearing process that is very effective.

He takes a walk after work reviewing how the day has gone, deciding what mistakes he's made, what to do about it and what to do differently next time. Then he releases any negative thoughts or guilt remaining about his mistakes.

In other words, he concentrates on correcting his mistakes rather than downgrading himself for making them in the first place.

Think now about what system you can put into place to accomplish these goals:

- Listen to your thoughts.
- Concentrate on correcting your mistakes.
- Hang on to the positive.
- Release the negative.

Could you allocate time each day as this top achiever does? Could you write down the positive? What steps can you take? Think about it as you read the next paragraphs.

ELIMINATING DOLDRUMS

The best way to eliminate doldrums is to take a moment to acknowledge yourself. Take time to acknowledge what you do right. Take time to acknowledge your persistence, your stamina, your determination, your progress in being organized, your sales skill building, and so on.

Watch children as a clue to human development. A two-year-old says, "I can do it, I can do it, I can do it." A three-year-old says, "I did it, I did it, I did it." They go from conviction, determination, and belief to success.

That's what you need to do too in creating success patterns. First, you have to have a positive attitude about the fact that you can do it, then you have to reinforce the fact that you have done it.

♦ Self-Motivation and Support Systems

That's the reason you have to stop to give yourself acknowledgment for your progress and success. Don't wait until you reach the end result because you'll get into the doldrums waiting. Acknowledge yourself for the small steps along the way.

For maximum success, write down your success steps and review them every evening or when you're most likely to get the doldrums.

Most people find it easier to criticize themselves than to acknowledge themselves. It comes from years of practice. Now is the time to reverse the process. When you acknowledge yourself, your morale will go up. And high morale is essential to keep yourself going.

Why not make a list now of skills and qualities you can acknowledge in yourself. Then you'll be able to refer to these when you need a morale boost.

Skills and Qualities

_____   _____   _____

_____   _____   _____

_____   _____   _____

_____   _____   _____

DARING TO BE DIFFERENT

Another top sales executive hired a secretary after being in insurance only six months. No one else was willing to be so daring. But he saw the potential of doing what he did best and delegating everything else. Now he has four members on his support staff and *ten times* the average income.

Chances are that you're holding yourself back from something. It may be hiring a secretary or trying a new method no one else uses. It might be investing in equipment or support staff, or doing presentations or demos a different way. Whatever it is, look again. Think again. Don't be afraid to be different.

Perhaps you will be an inspiration, not only for yourself but for others. There are plenty of mediocre salespeople doing things in their standard way. If you want to be successful you have to be determined, committed, positive, disciplined, and different.

Being different alone won't do it. But being different on top of being determined, committed, positive, and disciplined can put you on a new plateau.

Think now. What are you holding yourself back from? Jot it down. Now decide what you are willing to do about it. Focus on the long-term effect you'll create, not the short-term resistance to change from those around you.

♦ Self-Motivation and Support Systems

Think about the questions that follow.

♦ What are you holding yourself back from? _____
♦ What am I willing to do about it? _____
♦ What result could I expect? _____

OVERCOMING ROADBLOCKS

Most people see a number of roadblocks between themselves and their goal. It looks something like this:

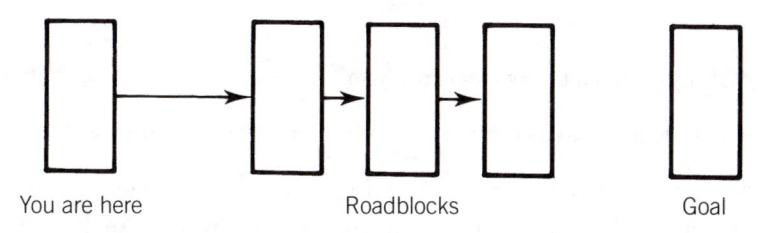

You are here   Roadblocks   Goal

The mentality shift that helps us overcome roadblocks is as straightforward as this:

Keep the goal in sight and focus determinedly on ways around the roadblocks.

It looks like this:

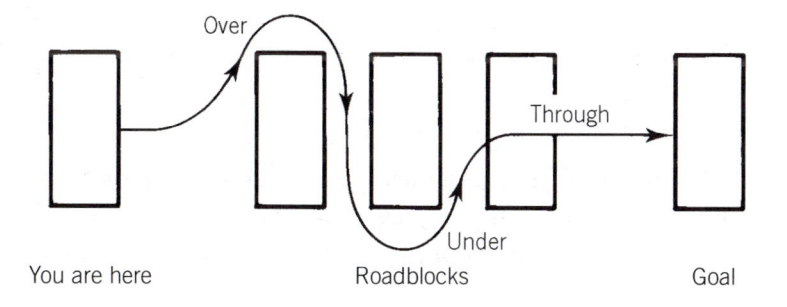

Over • Under • Through

You are here   Roadblocks   Goal

In reality, roadblocks are nothing more than challenges that help us grow. One person's roadblock is nothing to another person because they've already gained skills in that direction. So why not go in that direction to gain those skills as well?

MOVING SPEEDILY TOWARDS YOUR GOAL

Have you heard this important saying? "Happiness is directly proportional to the speed you're moving toward your goal."

Now, ask yourself these questions:

- What happens if I have no goal?
- If my goal isn't very clear in my mind?
- If I see my goal as one big chunk rather than daily pieces?

All of those actions leave you feeling that you're moving slower or not at all towards your goal. You get caught in a downward spiral.

What can you do every day to make sure you're creating an upward spiral, moving closer to your goal? The answer is to have your goal clearly defined, break it into action segments, and tackle the segments every day without fail.

When you develop that discipline, success will be in your hands. Without it, you're giving your power away. What is *your* clearly defined goal? What are the segments that will help you reach it?

CONSIDER YOUR PAST SUCCESSES

Think now of all your past successes. Think of your successes early in your career, early in your education. Think of any contest or competition you won, no matter how young you were.

◆ Self-Motivation and Support Systems

What quality did you have that helped you win? You still have it. Now is the time to harness this to help you overcome your roadblocks.

Every individual has a great deal more potential than they ever imagine. The goal or vision you have in your mind must be exactly right for you because no one else has that same vision. Don't let a simple roadblock stop you. Use your strengths to overcome it.

I'm behind you and I wish you success in your journey, every step of the way!

Remember, when you come to a crossroad
in life,
take the most challenging path.

Chapter 8

Summarizing Successful Selling

This book identifies ways to master seven critical areas of selling. Here is a summary of the "make or break" points of concentration:

PLAN YOUR SUCCESS (CHAPTER 1)

- Set overall goal
- Create daily segments
- Measure your results
- Mental readiness

GAINING PRODUCT AND SERVICE EXPERTISE (CHAPTER 2)

- Finding sources of knowledge
- Plan your strategy
- Attend training courses
- Implement your strategy

DISCOVER THE BUYING MOTIVES (CHAPTER 3)

- The correct way to find motives
- Check your assumptions

◆ Summarizing Successful Selling

- ◆ The time to present motives
- ◆ Present motives linked to benefits

OVERCOME OBJECTIONS (CHAPTER 4)

- ◆ The process
- ◆ Handling price objections
- ◆ Closing despite objections

PRESENTATIONS AND CLOSINGS (CHAPTER 5)

- ◆ *Ask* questions to determine the customer's corporate buying motive
- ◆ *Ask* questons to determine the customer's personal buying motive
- ◆ *Know* your product as an expert
- ◆ *Know* the competition's strength and weakness
- ◆ *Tell* about the links between their need and your benefits
- ◆ *Tell* how you overcome objections
- ◆ *Review* needs and benefits
- ◆ *Ask* for their decision

ACTION-PROVOKING SYSTEMS (CHAPTER 6)

- ◆ Computerized systems
- ◆ Manual systems for prospecting

SELF-MOTIVATION AND SUPPORT SYSTEMS (CHAPTER 7)

- Staying positive
- Eliminating doldrums
- Daring to be different
- Overcoming roadblocks

INDEX

Action provoking systems, 57–68, 83
  advantages, 59–61
  benefits, 59
  computerized systems, 62–63
  customer interest cycle, 58–59
  diary systems, weaknesses, 61–62
  manual systems for prospecting, 63–68
  work:
    hard, 59
    intelligently, 59
Assumptions:
  avoiding, 27
  checking, 25–27

Benefits:
  expressing, 15–16
  link to:
    motives, 29–30
    needs, 49–52
Businesses, new, 7–8
Buying motives:
  corporate, 46
  discovering, 21–31
    assumptions:
      avoiding, 27
      checking, 25–27
    benefits, link to motives, 29–30
    conversation, targeting, 23–24
    motives, presenting, 27–29
    needs assessment, 27–29
    psychological motives, 22–25
    questioning techniques, 24
  personal, 47

Calculating:
  targets, 6–8
  workload, 3

Charts, self-management, 9–10
Clarification questions, 40–41
Closings, 45–56
  benefits, link with needs, 49–52
  buying motives:
    corporate, 46
    personal, 47
  competition, knowledge of, 48–49
  decision, seeking, 54–56
  needs and benefits, reviewing, 53–54
  objections, overcoming, 42, 52–53
  product expertise, 37–38, 47–48
  questions, asking, 46–47
Coaching, 71
Competition, knowledge of, 48–49
Computerized systems, 62–63
Conversation, targeting, 23–24
Courses, training, 14, 19
Customer interest cycle, 58–59
Customers, interviewing, 15
Cycles, customer interest, 58–59

Daily:
  segments, 5–8
  targets, 5
Deception, self, 4–5
Decision, seeking, 54–56
Diary systems, weaknesses, 61–62
Doldrums, eliminating, 74–76

Expertise, gaining, 11–20, 82
  benefits, expressing, 15–16
  customers, interviewing, 15
  knowledge, sources, 14–16
  product expertise, 14
  responsibility, 13

self investment, 13
strategy, implementing, 19–20
strategy, planning, 16–19
training courses, 19

Goal:
progress, 78–79
setting, 2–5

Hard work, 59
Historical recording system, 62–63

Intelligent work, 59
Interest cycle, 58
Investing, yourself, 13

Knowledge, sources, 14–16

Learning, 12–20

Management systems, 9–10
Manual systems for prospecting, 63–68
Mental readiness, 10
Motivation, 69–79
coaching, 71
doldrums, eliminating, 74–76
goals, progress, 78–79
negative thoughts, 73–74
people, as supports, 72–73
positive attitude, 73–74
roadblocks, overcoming, 77–78
support, necessary, 71–72
Motives:
benefits, link to, 29–30
buying, discovering, 82–83
assumptions:
avoiding, 27
checking, 25–27
benefits, link to motives, 29–30
conversation, targeting, 23–24
logical, 25
needs assessment, 27–29
presenting, 27–29
psychological, 22–25
questioning techniques, 24
presenting, 27–29

Needs:
and benefits, 49–51
reviewing, 53–54
assessment, 27–29
Negative thoughts, 73–74

Objections, overcoming, 33–44, 52–53, 83
clarification question, 40–41
closing, 42
explanation, 39–40
preparation, 43
price, 37–40
process, 35–37, 41
reference chart, 44
Obstacles, overcoming, 77–78
Opportunities, 8

People, as supports, 72–73
Planning success, 2–10, 82
businesses, new, 7–8
daily:
segments, 5–8
targets, 5
deception, self, 4–5
goal setting, 2–5
mental readiness, 10
opportunities, 8
reminders, making, 6
results, measurements, 8–10
self management systems, 9–10
shortfalls, predicting, 10
targets, calculating, 6–8
workload, calculating, 3
Positive attitude, 73–74
Preamble, overcoming objections, 35–37

Presentations, 45–56, 83
　benefits, link with needs, 49–52
　buying motives:
　　corporate, 46
　　personal, 47
　competition, knowledge of, 48–49
　decision, seeking, 54–56
　needs and benefits, reviewing, 53–54
　objections, overcoming, 52–53
　product:
　　expertise, 47–38
　　knowledge, 47–48
　questions, asking, 46–47
Price objections, 37–40
Process, overcoming objections, 35–37, 41
Product expertise, 12–20, 47–48, 82
Prospecting systems, 9–10, 63–68
Psychological motives, 22–25

Questioning techniques, 24, 46–47

Reminders, making, 6
Results, measurements, 8–10
Roadblocks, overcoming, 77–78

Sales, opportunities, 8
Self deception, 4–5
Self management systems, 9–10
Self motivation, 69–79, 84
　coaching, 71
　doldrums, eliminating, 74–76
　goals, progress, 78–79
　negative thoughts, 73–74
　people, as supports, 72–73
　positive attitude, 73–74
　roadblocks, overcoming, 77–78
　support, necessary, 71–72
Service expertise, 12–20, 82
Shortfalls, predicting, 10

Smart work, 59
Strategy:
　implementing, 19–20
　planning, 16–19
Success, planning, 2–10, 82
　businesses, new, 7–8
　daily:
　　segments, 5–8
　　targets, 5
　deception, self, 4–5
　goal setting, 2–5
　mental readiness, 10
　opportunities, 8
　reminders, making, 6
　results, measurements, 8–10
　self management systems, 9–10
　shortfalls, predicting, 10
　targets, calculating, 6–8
　workload, calculating, 3
Support, necessary, 71–72
Support systems, 69–79, 84
　coaching, 71
　doldrums, eliminating, 74–76
　goals, progress, 78–79
　negative thoughts, 73–74
　people, as supports, 72–73
　positive attitude, 73–74
　roadblocks, overcoming, 77–78
　support, necessary, 71–72
Systems:
　action provoking, 57–68
　computerized, 62–63
　diary, 61–62
　manual, for prospecting, 63–68

Targets, calculating, 6–8
Training courses, 19

Uniqueness, 76–77

Work:
　hard, 59
　intelligently, 59
Workload, calculating, 3